Oscar

John Escott

 Richmond READERS

Richmond READERS

LEVEL **1**

(500 headwords)

Maria's Dilemma

Oscar

Jack's Game

The Boy from Yesterday

The Black Mountain

LEVEL **2**

(800 headwords)

Jason Causes Chaos

Craigen Castle Mystery

The Road through the Hills and othes stories

Where's Mauriac?

Saturday Storm

LEVEL **3**

(1200 headwords)

A Trip to the Stars

Dr Jekyll and Mr Hyde

The Canterville Ghost and Other Stories

Cold Feet

Frankenstein

LEVEL **4**

(1800 headwords)

A Trip to London

Dracula

Jane Eyre

The Adventures of Tom Sawyer

Sense and Sensibility

LEVEL **5**

(2600+ headwords)

Steve Jobs: the man behind Apple

Elizabeth II The Diamond Queen

Oscar

Background Information: This story takes place in a small English town in the early 1930s. Mr Felberg makes clothes for men. He is a tailor. Joseph and Sidney work for him. Mr Felberg is teaching them to make men's clothes. Joseph and Sidney are Mr Felbergs's apprentices. After five years, they can become tailors like Mr Felberg.

....

John Escott writes books for students and young people. He lives in Bournemouth, by the sea. He is married and has two children and two young grandchildren.

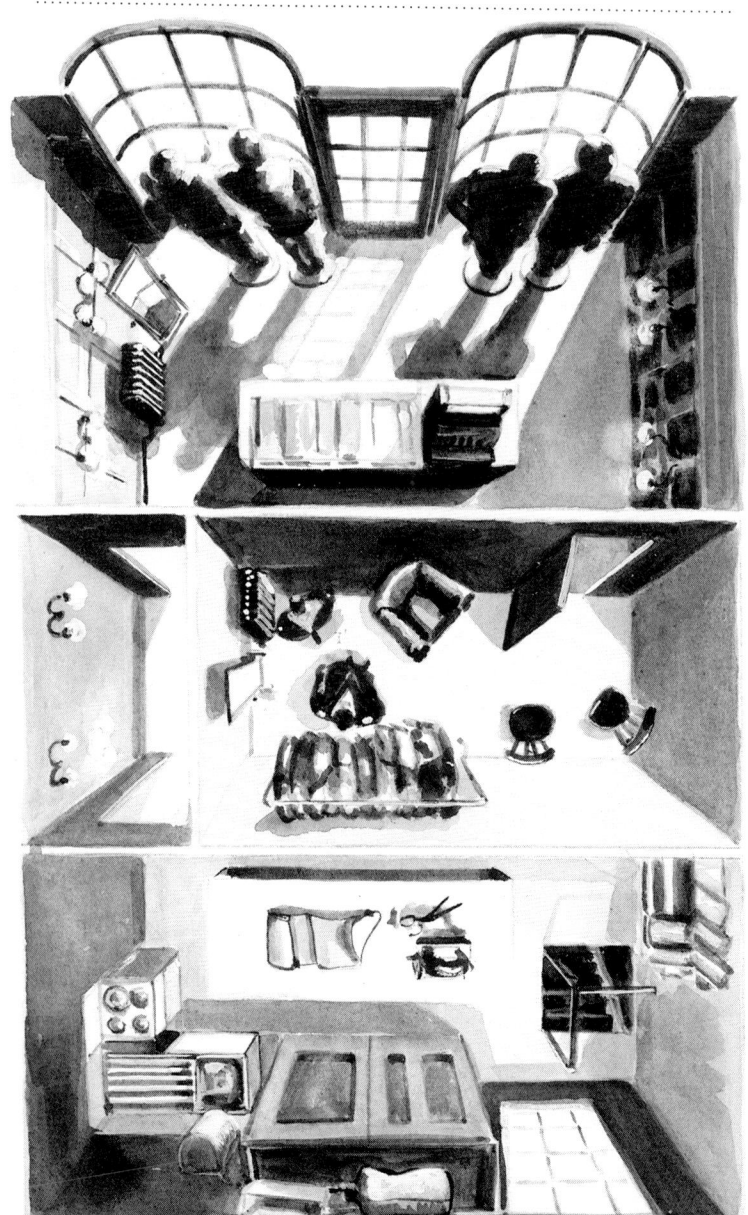

Mr Felberg's shop

CHAPTER 1

Joseph's First Day

Joseph was fifteen, and it was his first day at Mr Felberg's shop.

'Today I am going to learn to make men's suits* with Mr Felberg!' he thought*. He was excited.

'Good morning, Mr Felberg,' Joseph said.

'Good morning, Joseph,' Mr Felberg said. 'We are pleased to see you. This is Sidney. He's twenty, and he works here too.'

'Hello,' Joseph said.

Sidney looked at Joseph but he did not answer. He moved away and put a coat on a window dummy.

'Good morning, Joseph,' Mr Felberg said. 'We are pleased to see you'.

'He does not like me,' Joseph thought. 'He does not want me to work here. Why?'

Mr Felberg took* Joseph to the back room.

'Now, what can I give you to do first, Joseph?' Mr Felberg said. 'Oh, yes. Put these four coats into this box. They are for an important client, and you can take them to him this morning.' He gave* Joseph a big box. 'Be careful* with them. Don't drop* them or make them dirty.'

'No, Mr Felberg,' Joseph said.

Sidney listened in the shop. His face was dark and angry.

A client came into the shop and Mr Felberg came out of the back room to see him.

'Good morning,' he said, and he smiled* at the client. 'What can we do for you?'

'I would like you to make me a suit,' the man said.

Sidney waited for Mr Felberg to take the client into the fitting room. Then he went to the room at the back of the shop.

Joseph began* to put the last coat into the box. Sidney hit Joseph's arm when he walked by, and Joseph dropped the coat.

'Sorry,' Sidney said. 'It was an accident.' He looked at the coat. 'That coat is dirty now. You can't take it to the client.'

'But...' Joseph began.

'You have to be careful with the coats and trousers here,' Sidney said. 'Didn't Mr Felberg tell you?'

Sidney hit Joseph's arm when he walked by, and Joseph dropped the coat.

After a minute or two, Mr Felberg came into the back room.

'What is happening?' he said.

'Joseph dropped a coat,' Sidney said. 'It's dirty now.'

Mr Felberg was angry. 'I said be careful!' he said to Joseph. 'Do you want to work here? Well, be careful!'

'I ... it was an accident,' Joseph said. His face was very red.

Sidney went back into the shop.

He smiled, but it was not a nice smile.

CHAPTER **2**

Joseph Meets Oscar

At one o'clock, Mr Felberg closed the shop.

'Come back at two o'clock,' he said to Joseph. 'You can go and have your lunch now.'

Joseph went to the park. He sat* under a tree to eat his lunch. After three or four minutes, he saw Sidney go into a small café across the road. There was a girl with him, and they laughed together.

'Sidney has got a girlfriend,' Joseph thought.

Joseph liked working at Mr Felberg's shop, but he did not like Sidney.

He watched the birds in the park, and gave them some of his lunch. Then he walked through the trees to the river. The sun was hot, and it was a beautiful day.

At two o'clock, Joseph went back to the shop. Sidney got back a minute or two after him.

'This afternoon, you can watch me. I am going to cut* the cloth to make a suit,' Mr Felberg said to Joseph. 'Where are the big scissors?'

'I put them on the work table this morning, Mr Felberg,' Joseph said.

'They are not there now,' Mr Felberg said. 'Where are they? I need them quickly.'

'I don't understand it,' Joseph said. 'They were there a minute ago.'

'Here they are, Mr Felberg,' Sidney said. 'They were

...he saw Sidney go into a small café across the road. There was a girl with him, and they laughed together.

in the cupboard.'

'But I thought I put them...' Joseph began.

'Please remember things, Joseph,' Mr Felberg said, and he went from the back room into the shop. He was angry.

Joseph looked at Sidney. 'You took the scissors from the table and put them in the cupboard,' Joseph said.

'Did I?' Sidney said, smiling. 'Why do you think I did that?'

'Because you want to make things difficult for me,' Joseph said. 'You want Mr Felberg to be angry with me. You don't want me to work here, do you?'

'Don't I?' Sidney answered.

'You don't want me to work here, do you?'

'No,' Joseph said. 'But why? Why don't you want me here?'

Sidney did not answer.

'Joseph!' Mr Felberg called from the shop. 'Go down to the cellar and get the blue cloth for Mr King's suit. He is going to come into the shop this afternoon, and I want him to see it.'

'Yes, Mr Felberg,' Joseph said.

He went down the stairs to the cellar under the shop. There were a lot of boxes in the cellar, and there was a window dummy in the corner. It was old and dirty, but Joseph smiled at the dummy's face.

Then he found* the blue cloth for Mr King's suit, and carried it back up the cellar stairs and into the shop.

'Thank you,' Mr Felberg said. He was not angry now. 'Thank you, Joseph. I am getting old. I don't like walking up and down the cellar stairs.'

■ ■ ■

'There's an old window dummy in the cellar,' Joseph said. 'He's got a nice face.'

Mr Felberg smiled. 'That's Oscar,' he said.

Joseph laughed. 'Oscar?' he said.

'I call him Oscar,' Mr Felberg said. 'He's very old, too. I don't put him in the window now.' He looked across the shop at Sidney. 'You remember Oscar, don't you, Sidney?'

'I ... I don't like that dummy,' Sidney said.

'Why don't you?' Mr Felberg said. 'I can't understand

...there was a window dummy in the corner. It was old and dirty, but Joseph smiled at the dummy's face.

it. It's a window dummy, that's all.'

'I don't like it,' Sidney said again.

Joseph looked at Sidney's face. 'He's afraid of it!' he thought.

'Well, I'm going to put Oscar back in the shop,' Mr Felberg said. 'He can wear the brown suit, and stay in the shop. Mrs Davis didn't like the suit, and her husband didn't buy it. Do you remember? Well, Oscar can wear it. Go and bring Oscar up from the cellar, Joseph.'

Joseph went down the cellar stairs again. He thought about Sidney's face.

'Why is Sidney afraid of an old window dummy?' he thought.

CHAPTER **3**

④

A One Pound Note

The next morning, Mr Felberg went out.

'I'm going to take a suit to Mr Baxter in Green Street,' he said to Sidney. 'You can stay in the shop.' He looked at Joseph. 'Joseph, there are some boxes in the back room. Take them down to the cellar. After that, you can clean the shop window.'

'Yes, Mr Felberg,' Joseph said.

Joseph went into the back room. He carried the boxes down the cellar stairs. He was very careful.

'I don't want to fall* down,' he thought. 'There are a lot of stairs!'

He put the boxes in the dark cellar. Then he went back up the cellar stairs to the room at the back of the shop. There was a sink under the window, and there was a bucket under the sink. Joseph put some water in the bucket.

'Now I must clean the shop window,' he thought.

He looked through to the shop and saw Sidney put something into his coat pocket. It was a one pound note. There was no one in the shop, and Sidney smiled.

'Where did Sidney get a one pound note?' Joseph thought. 'Did he take it from the till*?'

Then Sidney stopped smiling. He looked across the room at something, and his face changed. Now he was afraid!

'What is he looking at?' Joseph thought. He moved near to the door of the back room. 'He's looking at Oscar!'

It was true. Sidney looked at Oscar ... and the dummy looked back at Sidney!

'Is Oscar watching Sidney?' Joseph thought. 'Can a dummy watch someone?'

He carried the bucket of water into the shop.

Sidney quickly looked away from the dummy and saw Joseph.

'What are you doing?' he said.

'I'm going to clean the shop window,' Joseph said.

'Do it, then!' Sidney shouted*.

He looked through to the shop and saw Sidney put something into his coat pocket. It was a one pound note.

Joseph carried the bucket of water out of the shop and began to clean the window. Sidney watched him. His face was angry.

■ ■ ■

Later, Joseph went to the park again to eat his lunch. It was hot in the sun and he went to sleep. When he opened his eyes, it was nearly two o'clock.

Joseph walked quickly along the street. He did not want to be late back to the shop.

'Mr Felberg will be angry,' he thought.

There was a market that day, and a lot of people were at the market. It was difficult to get past all the people.

'Excuse me!' Joseph said. 'Please, can I get through?'

Then he saw Sidney.

The young man was with the girl again. They were at a market stall. The man behind the market stall smiled. Joseph saw him give something to the girl. It was a green brooch.

'Do you like it?' Sidney said to her.

'Oh, yes!' she said.

'Then you can have it!' Sidney said, laughing.

And he gave the man a one pound note.

Joseph saw him give something to the girl. It was a green brooch.

CHAPTER **4** ⑤

Mr Felberg is Angry

It was the middle of the afternoon the next day. Sidney was in the shop.

He looked into the back room. Mr Felberg cut some cloth and Joseph watched him. Sidney saw that the boy was interested in the work and wanted to learn.

'But I don't want him to stay,' Sidney thought. 'That boy sees things. There are some things that I don't want him to see.'

17

A moment later, Sidney went across to the till and opened it quietly. There were three one pound notes in the till. Sidney took one of them out, and put it into his pocket ... and was suddenly* cold all over his body*.

He looked up quickly.

'Somebody is watching me!' he thought.

But there was no one in the shop, and Mr Felberg and the boy were in the back room.

'Oscar!' Sidney thought. And he looked across at the dummy. 'Oh!'

Oscar's hard, black eyes looked at Sidney.

'Can he see things? Is ... is he real?' Sidney thought. 'No, that's impossible! But...'

After a moment, Sidney took the one pound note out of his pocket.

'Why am I doing this?' he thought.

And he put it back into the till.

■ ■ ■

'Boy!' Sidney shouted, the next morning. 'Come here!'

Joseph walked into the shop from the back room.

'What are you doing in there?' Sidney asked him.

'I'm cutting some cloth,' Joseph said. 'Mr Felberg asked me to cut it before he comes back.'

Mr Felberg was at an important client's house.

'Oh,' Sidney said. He thought for a moment, then he said, 'Go to the shop down the road and get me a newspaper. Here's some money.'

'A newspaper?' Joseph said, surprised. 'Why do you

want a newspaper?'

'Don't ask questions!' Sidney shouted. 'Do it!'

Joseph took the money and went to the newspaper shop down the road. He came back five minutes later.

A moment or two after this, Mr Felberg came back.

'Did you finish cutting that cloth for me, Joseph?' he asked.

'It's nearly ready, Mr Felberg,' Joseph said.

The old man went into the back room with Joseph. Sidney watched them and smiled. He waited. A moment later, Mr Felberg began to shout.

'No, no, no! This is not right!' he shouted. 'What did you do? You cut it all wrong.'

'But I didn't...' Joseph began.

'No, no, no! This is not right!' he shouted. 'What did you do? You cut it all wrong.'

'This is expensive cloth, and now I can't make anything with it!' Mr Felberg shouted. 'I said be careful with it. Now look at it!'

'It wasn't me, Mr Felberg!' Joseph said. He looked at Sidney in the shop. 'It was him! It was Sidney! I went to get him a newspaper, and...'

'What!' Sidney shouted. 'What are you saying? It's not true! I didn't...'

'Stop!' Mr Felberg said. 'Stop it! Don't say another word.' The old man looked at Joseph. 'Maybe this is the wrong job for you, Joseph. Maybe you would like to look for another job.'

'No!' said Joseph. 'I like it here, Mr Felberg. I'm sorry about the cloth, but...'

'All right! But be more careful the next time,' Mr Felberg said. 'Now, go and have your lunch. It's nearly one o'clock.'

Sidney watched Joseph go out of the shop, then he said, 'He's the wrong boy for this job, Mr Felberg. We don't need him here.'

'Maybe you are right, Sidney,' the old man said. 'Maybe you are right.'

Sidney smiled ... and then went cold all over his body. He looked across at Oscar and saw the dummy's eyes watching him. The eyes were dark and angry, and Sidney was suddenly very afraid.

The Dummy Must Go!

A week went by. Sidney was afraid to come to work at Mr Felberg's shop. It was all because of that dummy! Oscar.

Why did it have a name? Why did the old man give it a name? It was only a dummy.

But Sidney knew* that this was not true. Oscar was not only a dummy.

'Dummies can't watch people,' Sidney thought. 'But he ... it ... watches me.'

It was true. Sidney knew that the dummy watched him every time he shouted at Joseph. He knew that it watched him every time he put his hand in the till.

He watched the dummy from the room behind the shop. Mr Felberg and Joseph were in the shop with a client. The client looked at Oscar's suit.

'It is the best cloth,' Mr Felberg said. 'Brown is a good colour for you, Mr Watts.'

'It looks good on your dummy,' the man said, smiling.

'On Oscar?' Mr Felberg said. 'Everything looks good on Oscar! That's right, isn't it, Joseph?'

'Oh, yes!' Joseph said.

And they all laughed.

'I would like to think about it and come back later,' Mr Watts said, after a moment.

'That's all right,' Mr Felberg said.

Sidney watched them from the back room. He did not like Joseph. The boy watched him all the time, and he always moved quietly through the shop. How much did he know? How much did he see?

And how much did Oscar know? How much did Oscar see?

Later that morning, Mr Felberg said, 'I can't find a one pound note. It was in the till this morning. That's the second time this week...'

'Maybe you gave it to a client,' Sidney said quickly. 'Yes, that's right. You gave it to that woman, this morning. She gave you a five pound note and you gave her the one pound note. Do you remember?'

'Did I?' Mr Felberg said. 'Oh, I am getting old! I can't remember things.'

Sidney began to smile. But then he looked across at Oscar, and he stopped smiling. The dummy's eyes were angry.

■ ■ ■

It happened that afternoon.

Sidney was in the shop, and Mr Felberg and Joseph were in the back room. A man came into the shop. It was Mr Watts.

'I want to buy that suit on your dummy,' Mr Watts said. 'I was here this morning.'

'Oh, yes,' Sidney said. 'I remember. Can you wait a moment, Mr Watts?'

Sidney went across to the dummy and began to take

the coat off it. Suddenly, the dummy's hand hit Sidney's arm - hard!

'Aaagh!' Sidney shouted.

Mr Felberg came from the back room.

Suddenly, the dummy's hand hit Sidney's arm - hard!

'What is it?' he said. 'What happened, Sidney?'

'It ... it hit me!' Sidney said.

'What hit you?' Mr Felberg asked.

'The ... the dummy,' Sidney said.

'Oscar?' Mr Felberg said, and began to laugh.

'It's true!' Sidney shouted. 'It hit my arm, and...'

'Go into the back room, Sidney,' Mr Felberg said. 'I can get Mr Watts' suit for him.'

'But...' Sidney began.

'Go into the back room!' Mr Felberg said. He was angry now.

Sidney went into the back room.

'What's the matter?' Joseph asked Sidney. 'Are you ill? Your face is all white.'

'What's the matter?' Sidney said quickly. 'Nothing! Nothing at all! Don't stop your work!'

But Sidney was afraid.

'That dummy must go!' he thought.

CHAPTER 6

The Cellar Stairs

It was midnight. The street was dark and quiet. Sidney put his key into the shop door. He opened the door. He looked up and down the street. Then he went quickly and quietly into the dark shop.

He waited for a moment.

Sidney put his key into the shop door.

'Can I do it?' he thought. 'I must do it!'

He saw Oscar. The dummy was in a grey suit now.

Sidney moved slowly across the shop, his hands in front of him.

The dummy watched him, its eyes moving.

Sidney put his hands on the dummy. 'Do it!' he said. 'Do it!'

He was afraid, but he carried the dummy across the shop. He carried it through the back room and across to the top of the cellar stairs. Now Sidney looked at the dummy and smiled. 'What am I going to do with you?' he said. 'Do you know?' He laughed. 'I'm going to push* you down these stairs!'

He looked at the dummy's face. The dummy's eyes looked back at him. The eyes were hard and black. There was life in those eyes. Once again, Sidney thought, 'This is not only a dummy! It's something ... real!'

'No!' he shouted. 'I must not think that!'

He began to push the dummy – but then, suddenly, the dummy began to push Sidney!

'No!' Sidney shouted. 'No, no! Stop! Please...!'

Then Sidney began to fall down the stairs.

The last thing he saw was Oscar's face ... laughing at him. Then he hit his head on the bottom stair, and everything went black.

■ ■ ■

Mr Felberg came to the shop early the next morning.

'Where is Oscar?' he thought.

Joseph came in at that moment. 'Good morning, Mr Felberg,' he said.

'Good morning, Joseph,' Mr Felberg said. 'Where is Oscar? Do you know?'

'No,' Joseph said, surprised.

They walked into the back room – and saw Oscar at the top of the cellar stairs.

'What...?' Mr Felberg began.

'Look!' Joseph said. 'Oscar is ... smiling!'

It was true. There was a big smile on the dummy's face.

He began to push the dummy - but then, suddenly, the dummy began to push Sidney!

Sidney was at the bottom of the stairs. His eyes were open, but he said nothing.

They went quickly across to the cellar stairs and looked down.

Sidney was at the bottom of the stairs. His eyes were open, but he said nothing. His left leg was under his body and his face was dark and afraid.

'Sidney!' Mr Felberg said, moving quickly down the stairs. 'What happened? Your leg ... did you break it?'

At first, Sidney did not answer. He looked at the dummy and his eyes did not move away from it. At last he said, 'Oscar ... he ... pushed me.'

The old man looked at him. 'Pushed you?' he said.

'Oscar can't push people, Sidney. He's only a dummy!'

Joseph looked at Oscar's smiling face.

'Is he?' he thought.

■ ■ ■

Sidney did not work at Mr Felberg's shop after the 'accident'. He was afraid to come back again.

After this, Mr Felberg did not 'forget' things anymore. And there was always the right money in the till.

And Oscar?

Oscar went back to the cellar.

'I think he is happier down there,' Joseph said to Mr Felberg.

'And how do you like it here, in my shop, Joseph?' Mr Felberg asked. 'You are working very well.'

Joseph smiled. 'I like it very much ... now,' he said.

'Thanks to Oscar!' he thought.

And Oscar? Oscar went back to the cellar.

EXERCISES

A Comprehension

Chapter 1 Write answers to these questions.

1 Mr Felberg tells Joseph to be careful with something. What?
2 What is the 'accident' that happens?

Chapter 2 Who said these words?

1 'Sidney has got a girlfriend.'
2 'They were in the cupboard.'
3 'Why don't you want me here?'
4 'I don't put him in the window now.'

Chapter 3 Who in this chapter...

1 put a one pound note in his pocket?
2 went to sleep in the sun?
3 gave a girl a green brooch?

Chapter 4 Are these sentences true (T) or false (F)?

1 Oscar took three one pound notes from the till.
2 Sidney was at an important client's house.
3 Joseph went to get a newspaper.
4 Sidney saw the dummy watching him, and was afraid.

Chapter 5 Find answers to these questions.

1 Why was Sidney afraid to come to work?
2 What could Mr Felberg not find?
3 What suit did Mr Watts want to buy?

Chapter 6 Who in this chapter...

1 ...was in a grey suit?
2 ...fell down the cellar stairs?
3 ...did not 'forget' things any more?

B Working with Language

1 Answer these questions with complete sentences.

Example: What did Mr Felberg do?
      He made men's suits.

Chapter 1   Why did Joseph drop the coats?
Chapter 2   Where did Joseph find the dummy?
Chapter 3   What did Sidney do at the market?
Chapter 4   Why did Mr Felberg shout at Joseph?
Chapter 5   What did Oscar do to Sidney?
Chapter 6   Why did Sidney go to the shop at midnight?

2 Use these words to join the sentences together.

before   and   to   but

1 Joseph liked working at Mr Felberg's shop. He did not like Sidney.
2 'Go down to the cellar.' 'Get the blue cloth for Mr King's suit.'
3 'I'm going to take a suit.' 'Mr Baxter in Green Street.'
4 'Mr Felberg asked me to cut it.' 'He comes back.'

C Activities

1 You are Joseph. Write a short letter to your sister, describing your first day at Mr Felberg's shop.
2 The day after the end of this story, Sidney's girlfriend visits him in hospital. She asks about his leg. Imagine their conversation and write a short dialogue.

GLOSSARY

began *(v)* past tense of *begin*

body *(n)* all of a physical person – everything you can see and touch

careful *(adj)* if you are careful, you do something with a lot of thought because you do not want to do it wrong

cut *(v)* to divide or separate something with a knife or scissors

drop *(v)* by accident, to let/make something fall* from your hands

fall *(v)* to suddenly* move down towards the ground

found *(v)* past tense of *find*

gave *(v)* past tense of *give*

knew *(v)* past tense of *know*

push *(v)* to move something away from you quickly and strongly with your hands

sat *(v)* past tense of *sit*

shout *(v)* to speak with a loud voice

smile *(v)* to make a happy face

suddenly *(adv)* if something happens *suddenly*, it happens very quickly

suit *(n)* a coat/jacket and trousers that you wear together

thought *(v)* past tense of *think*

till *(n)* a container in a shop where you keep money

took *(v)* past tense of *take*